Move

Julia Taudevin

T0348074

methuen | drama

LONDON • NEW YORK • OXFORD • NEW DELHI • SYDNEY

METHUEN DRAMA
Bloomsbury Publishing Plc
50 Bedford Square, London, WC1B 3DP, UK
1385 Broadway, New York, NY 10018, USA
29 Earlsfort Terrace, Dublin 2, Ireland

BLOOMSBURY, METHUEN DRAMA and the Methuen
Drama logo are trademarks of Bloomsbury Publishing Plc

First published in Great Britain 2021

Cover design by Tjasa Krivec

Photography by Sandie MacIver/Artwork by Brian Hartley

A catalogue record for this book is available from the British Library.

A catalog record for this book is available from the Library of Congress.

ISBN: PB: 978-1-3502-9190-4
ePDF: 978-1-3502-9191-1
eBook: 978-1-3502-9192-8

Series: Modern Plays

Typeset by Mark Heslington Ltd, Scarborough, North Yorkshire

To find out more about our authors and books visit
www.bloomsbury.com and sign up for our newsletters.

Disaster Plan in association with Slung Low and
the Traverse Theatre presents

MOVE

by Julia Taudevin

An earlier version of this text was produced by Disaster Plan and sruth-
mara in association with An Lanntair under the title *Move~Gluasad* and first
performed at Kinloch Community Hub, Isle of Lewis on Monday 27 January
2020.

The premiere production of Move was first presented by Disaster Plan in
association with Slung Low and the Traverse Theatre at Silverknowes Beach,
Edinburgh 3-7 August 2021, as part of the Made In Scotland showcase.

Cast

Nerea Bello

Helen Katamba

Mairi Morrison

Beldina Odenyo

Julia Taudevin

Creative Team

Written and directed by Julia Taudevin

Songs collected from the oral tradition

Sound devised by the company and arranged by Julia Taudevin

Dramaturg: Kieran Hurley

Transfer Director: Alan Lane

Sound Designer: Matt Angove

Costume Designer: Catherine Barthram

Producer: Luke Holbrook

Producer, Slung Low: Joanna Resnick

Stage Manager: Nia Wood

Image: Photograph by Sandie McIver. Artwork by Brian Hartley

Additional photography by Brian Hartley

The production was subsequently streamed online via Traverse 3 from 24 August 2021, with the support of the following additional production team members

Director of Photography: Kirstin McMahon

Editor: Stevie Malloch

Sound Design: Heather Andrews

Focus-Puller: Lara Abrami

Sound Recordist: Matt Angove / Calum Deas

THE COMPANY

Julia Taudevin | Writer, Director, Cast

Julia is an award-winning writer, performer and director and is co-artistic director of Disaster Plan. Her plays include Dario Fo Festival Award winner and Edinburgh Fringe hit *Blow Off* and James Tait Black Award for Drama shortlisted *Some Other Mother*; she co-directed multi-award-winning theatre shows *Beats* and *Heads Up* both by Kieran Hurley; her first short film *Duck Daze* won Best Screenplay at Underwire 2019 and she has an original TV drama currently in development; she has worked as an actor for over twenty years for companies including the National Theatre, National Theatre of Scotland and the Traverse Theatre; she was the 2020 IASH – Traverse Theatre Creative Fellow at the University of Edinburgh and will be taking *Auntie Empire*, written during her fellowship, into development in the autumn.

Nerea Bello | Cast

Nerea Bello is a Basque singer/performer and researcher based in Scotland. She moves seamlessly between solo, collaborative and theatre work. Nerea is passionate about rediscovering forgotten sounds and unearthing old ways of singing; celebrating the sound of raw, unadulterated voices that can fearlessly express vulnerability and emotion. Projects include *Away with the Birds*, *Women of the Hill*, *Votive*, *Sing the Gloaming*, *Nomanslanding* and many more. Nerea's composition and use of music in performance was nominated for the Critics' Awards for Theatre in Scotland for *AMADA*, directed by Cora Bissett.

Helen Katamba | Cast

Theatre includes: *Lyceum Christmas Tales* (Lyceum Theatre), *Breakfast Plays: Matterhorn and Doomsdays* (Traverse Theatre), *Pinocchio* (Citizens Theatre), *The Ugly One* (Tron Theatre), *Macbeth* (National Theatre), *The Three Musketeers* (The Dukes Theatre), *A User's Guide to Mind Control* (Acrimony Hoax and Grody), *King Lear* (Royal Conservatoire of Scotland)

Film includes: *The Lost King*, *Wild Rose*

TV Includes: *The Nest*, *The Feed*, *Last Commanders*

Mairi Morrison | Cast

Mairi Morrison trained as an actress at the Royal Conservatoire of Scotland. She is also a professional singer and writer. She is a recipient of the New Playwrights Award from Playwrights' Studio, Scotland.

Theatre includes: *Bana-Ghaisgich, Scotties, Ceilidh, Shrapnel* (Theatre Gu Leòr), *Last Tango In Partick* (National Theatre of Scotland), *Dunsinane* (National Theatre of Scotland/Royal Shakespeare Company), *Briseadh na Cloiche*, (C 's C Productions), *Yellow on the Broom, Perfect Days, Whisky Kisses, The Admirable Crichton* (Pitlochry Festival Theatre), *Away with the Birds* (Trigger Stuff), *Angus: Weaver of Grass* (Horse + Bamboo Theatre), *A Dead Man's Dying* (Òran Mòr/NTS), *Jacobite Country, The Seer* (Dogstar Theatre), *Eat your Heart Out* (Òran Mòr).

Radio includes: *Rùintean Màiri Iain Mhòir, Danns a' Rathaid* (BBC & Theatre gu Leòr); *Room for Refugees – Farid, Mystery of the Hills* (BBC)

TV/Film includes: *Outlaw King, Bannan, Katie Morag, Briseadh na Cloiche, Dà Là san Damhair, Bad Brown Owl* and extensive voiceover credits.

Mairi is currently working on a new album and play.

Beldina Odenyo | Cast

Beldina Odenyo/Heir of The Cursed is a vocalist, poet and writer creating work between the fields of music and theatre. Her work attempts to explore the differences and kinship between her dual Kenyan and Scottish heritage through words, music and visual art.

Matt Angove | Sound Designer

Matt is Slung Low's Technical Director. He trained as a Sound Designer and Sound Engineer, specialising in Theatre and Live Performance.

He has been a part of Slung Low since 2008 when they created their show *Helium* starring Patrick Stewart and has been involved in every show since. In 2019, Slung Low created a partnership with The Holbeck, the oldest social club in the UK, which the company run as a pay-what-you-decide theatre and community space. During the 2020–1 Covid crisis they became a non-means tested food bank.

Catherine Barthram | Costume Designer

Catherine Barthram is a freelance costume maker. Catherine has worked with Glasgow Life on their touring pantomine, *Pester-Rossi* to make clothing for participatory performances, Company Many to bring an enormous floor cloth to life, and Barrowland Ballet to dress a troupe of amateur dancers for film.

Luke Holbrook | Producer

Luke is an independent Creative Producer and Dramaturg making new theatre and film with pioneering artists. He is Producer for Disaster Plan, alongside developing work with artists including Imogen Stirling, Ciara Elizabeth Smyth and Oisín Kearney. Luke was previously Programmer and Producer for Assembly Festival, curating an award-winning theatre programme at the Edinburgh Festival, and leading the year-round artistic programme at Assembly Roxy. Luke spent six years as a literary agent at Casarotto Ramsay and Associates, working with a prestigious list of writers, directors and literary estates. He is a trustee of award-winning visual theatre company Tortoise in a Nutshell.

Kieran Hurley | Dramaturg

Kieran Hurley is an award-winning writer for stage and screen. Theatre work includes *Hitch*, *Chalk Farm*, *Square Go*, and *Mouthpiece*. Screenwriting includes *Beats* (2019), adapted from his play of the same name. *The Enemy*, Kieran's adaptation of Henrik Ibsen's *An Enemy of the People* will be produced by National Theatre of Scotland later this year. With his partner and long-term collaborator Julia Taudevin, Kieran is co-artistic director of new alternative theatre outfit Disaster Plan.

Alan Lane | Transfer Director

Alan Lane is Artistic Director of Slung Low, directing most of their work over the last decade including projects with the Barbican, the RSC, The Almeida, West Yorkshire Playhouse, Liverpool Everyman, Sheffield Theatres, Singapore Arts Festival and the Lowry. Slung Low make large-scale people's theatre work on stages, trains, castles, swimming pools, fishing boats and town centres.

In 2017 Slung Low headlined Hull UK City of Culture 2017 with *Flood* by James Phillips: a four-part epic performed online, live and on the BBC.

Alan has directed in places as wide ranging as the National Theatre of Croatia, a sari shop in Manchester, Buckingham Palace and in a village in Purulia, Southern India.

He was the Artistic Director for the National Commemoration of the Centenary of the Battle of the Somme on 1 July 2016: a ceremony with a people's theatre company of 450.

Disaster Plan would like to thank the following for their help with this production: The City of Edinburgh Council, Edinburgh College, Edinburgh Festival Fringe Society, Federation of Scottish Theatre, MTP, No Drama, The National Theatre of Scotland, Silverknowes Golf Course (Edinburgh Leisure), Fiona Sturgeon Shea, Emma McKee, Hanna Tuuliki, Annie Grace, Florencia Garcia Chafuén, Henry Bell, Harry Wilson, Catrin Evans, Playwrights' Studio, Scotland and the local businesses and community at Silverknowes.

Special thanks to the team that created MOVE~GLUASAD, the performance that gave birth to MOVE, Anna Porubcansky, Caitlin Skinner, Ewan Downie, Maryam Hamidi, Neshla Caplan, Katharine Williams, Alicia Bruce, Elleanor Taylor, Andrew Eaton-Lewis, Matt Addicot, Allun Woodward, Sruth-Mara, Mischief La Bas, Company of Wolves, Platform Glasgow and An Lanntair

About Disaster Plan

Disaster Plan marks the beginning of a new formal identity for the long-term collaboration between Julia Taudevin and Kieran Hurley. Our past work together has produced award-winning and internationally acclaimed theatre shows such as *Hitch, Beats, Chalk Farm, Rantin, Heads Up* and *Blow Off*. We make accessible, exciting, cross-artform theatre for a diverse range of audiences across Scotland and beyond.

disasterplan.co.uk

About Slung Low

Founded in 2000 Slung Low is an award-winning theatre company specialising in making epic productions in non-theatre spaces, often with large community performance companies at their heart.

Slung Low created *Flood* by James Phillips, a year-long epic for Hull UK City of Culture told online, live in Hull and on BBC2. Over a half million people saw a part of *Flood* and the show won a Royal Television Society Yorkshire Award for excellence.

In 2016 Slung Low built a camp of artists who lived for a week in the grounds of the RSC working with visiting public to create a ceremony that attempted to open the portal to the fairy world.

Recent work – on an epic scale using cityscapes as backdrops – includes *Mapping The City* (with iMove Yorkshire Cultural Olympiad in Hull), *Blood and Chocolate*, (York Theatre Royal and Pilot Theatre), *The White Whale* (Leeds Inspired) and *Camelot: The Shining City* (Sheffield Theatres and Sheffield Peoples' Theatre).

The company manage The Holbeck in Leeds: the oldest working men's club in Britain. They run the bar as a traditional members' bar and the rest of the building as an open development space for artists and a place where Slung Low invite other companies to present their work that otherwise might not get to be seen in Leeds. All work presented at The Holbeck is Pay What You Decide. The equipment and vehicles of the company are lent to those who have need. It is a useful place that shares its resources with those artists who need them.

In autumn 2018 Slung Low launched a Cultural Community College based in Holbeck; a place where adults come to learn new cultural skills – from stargazing to South Indian cooking, from carpentry to singing in a choir – and all workshops, supported by Paul Hamlyn Foundation, are provided on a Pay What You Decide basis.

During the Covid crisis of 2020 the company was the ward lead for Holbeck and Beeston for social care referrals with responsibility for 7,500 homes. They ran a non-means tested self referral foodbank from March 2020 to June 2021: delivering 15,000 food parcels.

We believe that access to culture is a fundamental part of a happy life. We believe that actions, however small, can have a big impact. We believe that culture can change our world for the better.

We are uncompromising in our beliefs.

slunglow.org

About Traverse Theatre Company

As Scotland's new writing theatre, the Traverse Theatre is a dynamic centre for performance, experience and discovery. Enabling people across society to access and engage with theatre is our fundamental mission.

Our year-round programme bursts with new stories and live performances that challenge, inform and entertain. We empower artists and audiences to make sense of the world today, providing a safe space to question, learn, empathise and – crucially – encounter different people and experiences. We commission, produce and programme for existing and future audiences to offer new and exciting experiences for everyone, and our partnerships with other theatre companies and festivals enable us to present a wide range of innovative performances.

We are passionate about developing talent and embracing the unexplored, working with the newest and rawest talent – with an emphasis on the Scottish-based – and nurturing it to become the art, artists and performances that can be seen on our stages through a variety of creative learning and literary programmes.

The timely, powerful stories that start life on our stages have global impact, resulting in dozens of tours, productions and translations. We are critically acclaimed and recognised the world over for our originality and artistic risk, which we hope will create some of the most talked-about plays, productions, directors, writers and actors for years to come.

Find out more about our work: *traverse.co.uk*

Supported by:

 ·EDINBVRGH·
THE CITY OF EDINBURGH COUNCIL

The Traverse Theatre is funded by Creative Scotland and The City of Edinburgh Council, with additional support from The Scottish Government Performing Arts Venues Relief Fund.

Traverse Theatre (Scotland) is a Limited Company (SC076037) and a Scottish Charity (SC002368) with its Registered Office at 10 Cambridge Street, Edinburgh, Scotland, EH1 2ED.

Move

Note from the playwright

Move is a weaving together of stories and songs in a form that is inspired by traditional Celtic keening rituals. Keening is the action of wailing in grief for a dead person and has been documented in cultures across the world but Move's main reference point is Gaelic keening which I first became aware of through my family roots on the Isle of Lewis. I have some relatives still alive on Lewis who jokingly summon up the distinctive keening sound they remember from their childhoods, but the practice was so comprehensively erased there that very little formal documentation remains.

What does the loss of this ritual mean, in a world so full of suffering and grief? What does it even mean to mourn in a such a world? Who gets to mourn and how? Who gets to be mourned and who doesn't? And what would it mean to mourn more fully, more communally, more justly across literal borders as well as borders of culture, pain and loss?

The stories in this play are drawn largely from a mixture of folklore, testimony and personal experiences shared during a dedicated research project funded by the Playwrights' Studio Scotland which informed the show. They are stories of migration, stories of loss, stories of trauma, and stories of hope and renewal. This is an ensemble piece where the song, the sound and the stories are equally important to each other and has been collaboratively made by the whole company each of us bringing our own cultural experience which is reflected in the work.

Prologue

The space feels ritualistic.

Performer One *enters.*

Performer One   She stands at the edge of the sea and clutches a bag to her chest.

The sea.

The sea.

The seemingly endless sea.

She thinks of the waves stretching away from her toes. She imagines catching one and riding it around the coast of Scotland towards the Isle of Lewis. She imagines riding the wave across the North Atlantic, veering south at the first sight of New York, pushing off from Colombia and slipping back towards the Mediterranean. She imagines the wave squeezing past Egypt, out into the Indian Ocean, touching Myanmar. Drifting south, then east, skirting Australia and heading towards the Pacific.

The sea.

The seemingly endless sea.

She stands.

She clutches the bag to her chest, the skin of her knuckles as white as its plastic handles. She hadn't prepared for receiving the ashes and so this bag for life has become a bag for death. Even in this moment of grief she makes a mental note to separate this bag from the others so she doesn't get caught out weeping uncontrollably at the supermarket check out later.

She steps closer to the sea, her eyes fixed on the horizon. She feels the space between the sea and her approaching feet shrinking and growing.

She thinks of those who the sea has taken from her in her lifetime and before it. And she thinks of those the sea has taken from anyone over the vast expanse of time as people have moved across it from one piece of land to another.

Tell me.

She says as the space between the waves and her toes shrinks and grows and shrinks and grows.

Tell me.

She says.

And the space between them shrinks. And grows. And shrinks. And grows.

Tell me.

She says.

Tell me what you know.

Performer Two *starts to sing 'Hiondo Hionda', the song of the seals documented in Celtic folklore.*

> *HIONDO HIONDA*
> Hiondo hionda hiondo hiondara

Performers Three, **Four** *and* **Five** *gradually join in. The sound overlaps like gentle waves on the ocean. The* **Performers** *appear.*

Performer One *joins them in song and the sound builds.* **Performer One** *kneels and starts to keen. One by one the rest follow suit. The keening swells. The sound is solid, loud, unrelenting. It reaches a climax and then*

1. Baby One

Performer One *rises up and starts speaking over the others whose singing continues, evolving into the melody of 'Kilmarnock' as sung in the tradition of singing the psalms in Gaelic, hummed, la'd softly, overlapping like hopeful waves under the text.*

Performer One   Think of a rumble. Think of a rumble that has been constant for days. It stops and the sound of her mother's heart rate quickens. She feels her mother stretch her limbs. She hears voices from every direction. She judders as bodies bump against her mother and now her mother is standing and she feels her own head slip deeper, muscles tightening around her as she descends. She feels her mother's hands press against her as the familiar twist ripples through her mother's womb.

Performer Three   Lays alan ya hubibi.   يس الان يا حبيبي

Performer One   She hears her mother whisper. But her mother knows there's nothing either of them can do to stop this. She feels her mother bend over and lay a cloth on the ground, buffeted by bodies running past her, shouting, calling to her mother to

Performer Five/Performer Four/Performer Two   Bagoaz! / Nagl! / Le bateau part! / Korri! / Move!

Performer One   But her mother can't move. She feels her mother's muscles around her own head contract. She feels her mother squat and the pull and twirl and twist and birl of her mother harnessing the strength of endless mothers before her, pushing her down. Down. Down. Twisting and twirling and birling down into the light. And she feels air against her head and air against her eyes and air in her nose, the world licking the border of her as she slips out into her mother's hands, the wash of air freezing her bare skin, the roar of ocean filling her ears, the suck in the pit of her as her mother bites the chord, the scrape of cloth as her mother wraps it around her naked body, the brush of lips as her mother whispers into her head

Performer Three   Wadaeaan. 'iilaa al'abad.   وداعا إلى الأبد

Performer One   The burn of spray as her mother splashes into the ocean after the departing boat, the cry from people in the boat as her mother hurls her over the waves towards it, the rush of wind as she flies through the air, the clench of a stranger's hands around her, the swell of the boat on the waves and the howl of her mother left bleeding on the shore.

Performer Three *wails the final crescendo of the 'Kilmarnock' melody and then snaps into singing the Swahili lullaby 'Mwanangu La La' all light and hopeful.*

> *MWANANGU LA LA*
> Useni Komo shimaki wa mwanangu e
> La la

The **Performers** *pick up the la las from the song and they overlap in a new wash of sound under the text.*

2. Old Woman One

Performer Two   Think of an old woman standing at a bus stop. She holds her phone in her arthritic fingers and looks up at the bus stop display board. It blinks random orange letters and numbers all jumbled and impossible to understand.

A bus pulls up and the driver looks at her, eyebrows raised. It's not every day you get such a helpful driver. But she's not getting on. Not because this isn't her bus. But because she can't remember what she's doing here and where she is meant to be going.

Her phone pings. It's a message from her daughter. She holds the screen up close to her eyes to read the words. Her daughter always uses English. It makes her life very difficult.

Her daughter wants to know where she is. Why doesn't she just say that then? Dónde estás? It's not that hard is it? Not that she could say anything more specific than Glasgow which probably wouldn't go down very well with her daughter. Glasgow is quite a big place after all.

She looks around at this place she thought it was a good idea to come to, twenty years ago now. Twenty. People rush from one place to the next like shoals of fish. How do they all remember where they are going?

She looks back at the message from her daughter and slides her knobbly finger through the neat rows of laughter and tears and skulls and hands and rainbows. She presses a cloud with thunder and lightning. She presses a roaring wave. She presses the gleaming sun. She presses the little arrow and looks up to sky as the phone swoops its swooping sending sound.

She watches dark clouds roll across the sky and remembers what it's like to watch waves crashing from underneath the surface of the ocean.

She hears the phone ping and knows it will be her daughter texting back with three question marks and the one you use for shouting – she can't think what that's called right now.

She thinks about a song she heard once at one of these refugees are welcome coffee mornings. She met a woman who wasn't allowed to stay in this country anymore but who couldn't go back to her own country and the woman sang a lullaby in Swahili. She remembers it was the first and only time in the entire twenty years she's lived here that she regretted not being able to speak English. Because if she could she would have been able to understand the woman's translation of the song. Her granddaughter found the song on YouTube later and told her it was about sleeping like the fish at the bottom of the water.

How is it she can remember these things and not the important things like where she is meant to be going right now?

Performer Four *sings 'Mwanangu La La' and the wash of the la las harmonise joyfully with her melody.*

> MWANANGU LA LA
> La la
> Useni komo shi maki wa
> Mwanangu e
> La La mwanangu
> Si pala wani kumu sha mwanangu e
> La la
> Nitako kingia hatari
> Kipenzi we
> La la

As the song reaches its end a new song, a new wash of sound begins, the lapping of the word 'leis' and 'seòl' from the Gaelic waulking song 'Leis an Lurgainn'.

3. Young Woman One

Performer Five   Think of a young woman sitting on a verandah. She is drunk. Drunker than she has ever been. She sits barefoot on the cement floor and rubs the neck of a beer bottle over a weave of scars across her wrist. A Spotify ad comes on and rescues her from having to witness some white chick trying to twerk to Ed Sheeran. She grips the neck of the bottle tighter and imagines throwing it at these people. The glass shattering against their heads but there's no blood. For some reason in this little flight of fancy of hers they've still got their blue helmets on. Their shiny blue helmets bringing the peace of the UN to this troubled land . . .

Performer Two   Hey.

Performer Five   Oh God, dickhead alert. She wants to say 'no vacancies pal'. She wants to say 'I'm only here for the free beer'. She wants to say 'fuck off'. But instead she just moves that cold glass bottle back and forth over those old scars on her wrist.

Performer Two   You'll get used to it.

Performer Five   He has little piggy eyes and a crusty mouth and she is absolutely certain she would have told him to get in the sea if he'd even looked at her back home. Home. What even is that? It's not Scotland where her mother and her grandmother probably still are. She hasn't spoken to either of them in years. The pain was just too much. It isn't Colombia. She hasn't been back since they left when she was a kid. And it isn't like she's got herself a job that's going to offer her much opportunity to carve out a nice little expatriate lifestyle for herself. The world's war zones don't usually make it to the front cover of *Ideal Home* magazine. She looks at these idiots around her. What on earth was she thinking signing up to this shit? Evangelising peace and democracy as if it isn't all a fallacy designed to distract from either colonialism or capitalism, or both, the root cause of pretty much every single fucking political mess she can think of.

Performer Two   . . . you're in shock. It's a completely natural response. Go to a shrink and he'll tell you you've got PTSD. And you probably do. I mean, my first time wasn't on this scale. These guys really know how to deliver a body count.

Performer Five   She wants to say 'I'll deliver *you* to the body count'. She wants to say 'fuck off'. She wants to say 'Those bodies are people'. She wants to say . . .

Performer Two   Mega. Today was mega. Mega blood. Shit, man. Yeah. I reckon if this was my first time I'd have PTSD.

Performer Five   Mega. Okay. Mega blood is apparently what she has come here to work with. She can't even think what word she would use for 'mega blood' when speaking to the good people of Myanmar. Lots? Lots and lots of blood? Lots and lots and lots and lots and lots and lots and lots . . .

Performer Two   . . . I probably had PTSD after Baghdad so if you need someone who knows how you're feeling then I'm here for you. No strings attached.

Performer Five   Time begins to swirl. She tries to put the beer bottle down on the cement floor but the verandah is spinning. She pushes her hands against the cold cement. She looks down at those hands. She recognises them. But she can't feel them anymore. And now she's looking down at the back of her own head. The back of her own head looking down at the backs of her own hands on the floor. And now she's watching her head look up to look at this ugly white dude with his little piggy eyes and his crusty lips. His flaky skin. His white gold wedding ring.

Performer Two   . . . Just a little jiggyjig to get you back in your body and ready for work in the morning. We call it Emergency Sex. It's totally legit. Ask anyone here. You may not know this but ancient mourning rituals were actually very sexy occasions. Of course we've lost all those old rituals now but we still have the primal need to copulate when death is around.

Performer Five   She watches herself look away from him and from her elevated position above her own body she wills herself to get up and walk away from this creep because she knows fine well this kind of thing can get ugly pretty quickly. She says to her body to move! Move! Move! And her body does! YAS! She watches her hands push her body up into a crouching position and then use the wall to steady her as she stands. She watches herself step off the verandah.

Performer Two   Take your time. I'm a gentleman.

The sound evolves and now the mournful non-vocable refrain from 'Leis An Lurgainn' sings out in repetition 'oh hi, oh hò, oh hì'.

Performer Five   Her bare feet hit the sandy ground. The waves sing to her through the palm trees. One step after another and she is on the beach, the stars lighting up the ocean. Her eyes on the horizon, she heads for the water. She feels it lick her feet and suck away the sand under her toes.

She falls to her knees and digs her hands, her useless, pointless hands with their scarred wrists deep and brings them up, offering handfuls of the earth to. To what? To who? She pulls her hands back towards her nose and inhales. The salty scent fills the utter emptiness inside her.

Her mind is filled with the bodies from today. The blood of them. The meat of them. She's seen bloody death before. Back when she was a kid. Her dad. Her grandad. Her uncles. So much death.

She thinks of her mother taking her away from Colombia. She thinks of her gran who went with them to Britain and raised her while her mother worked so many hours on so many different jobs she might as well have been dead herself.

She thinks of her gran. And she digs her hands deeper into the sand. Her gran. Her gran who refuses to learn English even after twenty years. Who refuses to be anyone other than the woman who lost all the men in her life. But she has a living and breathing granddaughter right here if only she could see her. She is digging her hands so deep now she feels tiny shards of shell cut into her scarred wrists.

She thinks of her gran's grandson. Her own brother. His small body lost in the sea twenty years ago when they made the journey to Scotland. Her gran always told her she should know how he died. As if her not remembering every single detail of her childhood is some kind of personal failing. He drowned. That's all she knows. Somewhere in the middle of the Atlantic.

She thinks of the thousands of bodies his body joined on the ocean floor.

She thinks of all the books and films and plays that she sees links to on Facebook and Twitter about travelling over the sea, the beautiful, romantic sea, in search of somewhere safe. As if this is some hip new cultural zeitgeist and not what humanity has done for millions of years. As if the sea hasn't been one of the main villains in those stories. Because people die. And death is shit. And dying in the sea is cold and wet and dark.

And she pulls her hands up and in the light peeking through the palm trees from the party on the verandah behind her she watches her own blood drip gently onto the sand and she screams: what the fuck am I doing here?

The sound cuts out and from the silence and suddenly, joyfully all performers sing 'Leis an Lurgainn' together rejoicing in the rhythm of the traditional movement that accompanies the waulking song, a communal song sung whilst waulking (beating) cloth against a hard surface to shrink it.

LEIS AN LURGAINN

An cuan Èirinn o hì
Muir ag èirigh o hò
'S cha bu lèir dhuinn o hì
Nì fon ghrèin ach na neòil

Leis an Lurgainn o hì
Leis an Lurgainn o hò
Beul an anmoich o hì
S'fheudar falbh le cuid seòl

Seachad Àros o hì
Bha i gàbhaidh o hò
'N fhairge làidir o hì
Suas gu bàrr a chroinn-sgòid

Leis an Lurgainn o hì
Leis an Lurgainn o hò
Beul an anmoich o hì
S'fheudar falbh le cuid seòl

4. Goddess

The song ends and a drone begins.

Performer Five   Imagine a woman, standing on the banks of the river Nile, approximately ten thousand years ago.

Performer Three *appears and leads a chant in call and response.*

Performer Three   Have awe

Awe

For Isis

Awe

Goddess

Awe

The sole mistress

Have awe

Awe

Awe

Awe

She gave birth to the morning

Have awe

Awe

She gave birth to mourning

Have awe

Awe

Awe awe awe

The chant builds and becomes epic, expansive, the awes harmonise with each other. Over the top **Performer Three** *weaves a melody of hope and awe.*

Performer Four *begins to keen.* **Performer One** *and* **Performer Five** *and* **Performer Two** *and* **Performer Three** *join in the keening building it until it becomes wild, dramatic, ridiculous . . .*

5. Deranged Cats

Performer Two *appears and watches the keeners critically.*

Performer Two   They sound like a bag of deranged cats.

Performer Three   Imagine. A woman standing on the crest of a hill in the Scottish highlands. In the mid nineteenth century.

Performer Two   Oh my mother would hate that I've said that. Draoidheachd she always called it. Madness more like. 'Às aonais stiùir nam beò, tha na mairbh a' dol a dh' ionnsaigh beatha ris nach urrainn dhaibh tilleadh.' Bah. Pagan nonsense.

They'll be snivelling at her feet and praising her for being such a kind and good woman – even though none of them would probably know her if they met her in their soup. Look at them down there. All squeezing into those miserable four walls. I honestly can't see what the all the fuss is about, the sooner they clear this place the better.

I'll cut across the moor and be at the port by morning.

The keening crescendos for a moment.

Oh good grief, there they go again. They'll be berating her ungrateful children now. And I'll be top of the list of course. Ungrateful daughter that I am refusing to mourn my own mother. Sure mother's soul wouldn't listen if I did stay and join in with all the boo boo hooing. I've been saying for years we should just let them have the land for the sheep and take the chance to get off this hideous chunk of rock. Not that those screeching moggies down there would approve of that. All clinging to a dying era without giving a single thought to

the pain and suffering of what everyone else is trying to
leave behind.

Ah, but soon enough they'll all be made to stand on the
Sabbath and be shut up for good. Show me a nice man in a
kilt with a set of pipes and I will be front of the funeral
queue any day.

'Tha caoineadh a' cuir nar cuimhne brìgh nan daonna. Tha
e gar cuideachadh ar siùil a' thionndadh ri mara nam bròin.'
The keening helps us turn into the sea of grief? Sea of grief?
The back end of the cow speaks more sense.

The keening stops.

Performer Two   Ah good. They've shut up. So long mother.
Knowing you you'll probably hang around this place until
the only thing left to haunt is the wretched sheep
themselves. BAAAAAAA! That's one for the sheep!

Performer Two *disappears.*

Performer Three *and* **Performer Five** *stand and strike up a new
energetic drone on C.*

Performer Four *sings an Irish keen for a dead child quietly,
intimately.*

> KEEN
> Ch oin och oin
> Agus me liom fèin
> Oh a rùn
> Agus och oin, och oin

Performer One *starts to sing* 'The King has Landed at Knoydart'
*in pibroch, the vocalisation of the bagpipes which, in Scotland,
replaced keening as the sound of mourning.*

> THE KING HAS LANDED AT KNOYDART
> Ho ro ro te hum
> Ho ro ro ro tun
> Ho ro ro te hum
> Ho ro ro ro tun

> Te um de bray o te o bray hum
> Ho ro ro te hum
> Ho ro ro to tun

The keen builds in strength, struggling against the pibroch. The two traditions battle. The keen wins.

Performer One *disappears. There is a moment of silence.*
Performer Two *strikes up a ridiculous operatic note and*
Performers Three, **Four** *and* **Five** *join in playfully,*

11. Eulogy

Performer Four   Imagine. A woman. Standing at the front of a church in Queensland, Australia. 1980s.

Performer One *walks awkwardly in front of the audience who is now the congregation gathered for her sister's funeral.*

Performer One   It's good to see so many of you here today. Margaret would have been chuffed I'm sure. Um. It's a real honour to be asked to speak. Because. Y'know, we weren't exactly the closest of sisters. But as probably most of you know, I was with her at the end.

I know it's all come as a bit of a shock for everyone. Forty-seven is not really that good an innings. Not even in cricket. But. Um. She used those forty seven years well. She was very good at . . . um . . . Pineapple Chicken. Lamingtons. And, um, you know, those celery sticks with peanut butter on them and little raisins on the top. What do you call that? Like frogs on a log or something? Never been a fan myself. But. Made a good buffet. That was Margaret. Good buffet maker.

And obviously she had a lot of friends. Lots of you here today to say goodbye. She was um. She was good at talking. Always better than me at that. Always better than me was my big sis. A real talker.

At the end there though, she had lost quite a lot of her words. Well, her English words. She still had the Gaelic, as she would call it. I had my sixth birthday on the boat when we moved here. So Margaret would have been just eight. And, um, I don't know. Those few years between us meant that she kept the Gaelic, and I didn't.

So there she was the other week giving it all hipdy hoori hooori hoori as they load her into the ambulance. And all the ambulance guys, the ambos are just rolling their eyes at me as if to say 'she's really lost it, yeah'? And, I mean, I know it wasn't gibberish but I only know how to say slainte mhor. Which, for the non Gaels amongst us means up your bum.

So yeah. There I was. My big sister dying, as it turns out, and these two ambos giving it all 'this nut's truly cracked'. And I say to them, 'No! No, that is the language of my ancestors'. And then of course, they say 'well what is she saying then?' And I don't know. I don't know what she was saying. So. Um. Sorry kids. I've let you down.

Well. No. Your mum has let you down really. Because I asked her so many times when we were kids to teach me my indigenous language. And she basically told me to go and bite my bum.

So. What do you want me to do? Make it up? Um. She was saying that she. Um. Loves you. And. Um. Stay in school. Get a job. And um. Don't marry a dickhead like your father. Sorry Jimbo.

Those were her last words, kids. Wasn't she great? Best big sister you could ever have asked for. Listened to everything you would say. With respect. And loving care. Never, ever, was like a real bitch to you. Or laughed at you and made jokes at your expense. Or stabbed you in the back. Or was like really, really mean to you. Never. Never did that. No. Not you Margaret. You were top notch! Here's to you. So long. And um. Thanks for all the memories.

Performer Two *sings 'An Ataireachd Ard', a Gaelic song about sailing the sea and leaving loved ones behind, purely, sincerely.*

> AN ATAIREACHD ARD
> An ataireachd bhuan
> Cluinn fuiam na h-ataireachd ard
> Tha torunn a'chuain
> Mar chualas leams' e'n am phaisd
> Gun mhuthadh gun truas
> A' sluaisreadh gainneimh na tragh'd
> An ataireachd bhuan
> Cluinn fuiam na h-ataireachd ard
>
> 'S na coilltean a siar
> Cha 'n iarrain fuireach gu brath
> Bha m'inntinn 's mo mhainn
> A riamh air lagan a' bhaigh
> Ach iadsan bha fial, an gniomh
> An caidreamh, 's an agh
> Air sgapadh gun dion
> Mar thriallas ealtainn roimh namh
>
> Ach siubhlaidh mi uat
> Cha ghluais mi tuilleadh 'n ad dhail
> Tha m'aois 'us mo shnuadh
> Toirt luaidh air giorrad mo la
> An am dhomh bhi suainnt'
> Am fuachd 's an cadal a' bhais
> Mo leabaidh dean suas
> Ri fuaim na h-ataireachd ard
> Na h-ataireachd ard

6. Old Woman Two

Performers One, **Four** and **Five** *return again to the 'la la' refrain from 'Mwanangu La La'.*

Performer Four *stands in the centre of the space, embodying the old woman from the three central stories.*

Performer Two   Remember the old woman at the bus stop. Think of her there with her phone still clasped to her chest. Her phone rings. She peers at the picture of her daughter on the screen and eventually presses her arthritic finger against the green.

Performer Three   Mamá. Where are you?

Performer Two   Her daughter asks. She looks around her but she doesn't know.

Performer Three   I need to come and get you.

Performer Two   She hates this English. It is such a heavy language.

Performer Three   Ha habido una masacre en Myanmar. Dónde estás?

The sung la las warp and distort, the notes elongating and clashing against each other. **Performer Four** *gradually falls to her knees, and pushes her hands into the ground.*

Performer Two   Her daughter's words sound far away all of a sudden.

Mayanmar. Where her granddaughter is. She was so scared when she heard her granddaughter had gone there. But she couldn't say anything. Not after years of silence. So she told herself that working with the UN would be good for her granddaughter. Make her less angry. Less unreachable. Less righteous.

But now this.

More death? She doesn't have the space in her heart to hold more deaths. It is still limp from the last one. Twenty years ago. She think of her grandson. His small body lost somewhere between here and Colombia. Twenty years. She imagines what he would look like now. A young man with bony shoulders and wide cheekbones and deep dark eyes. Just like his grandfather. And his uncles. So much death.

She drops the phone from her ear and looks around her. She is no longer at the bus stop. Lights spin and cars swirl. Swarms of people part and swerve around her as she she staggers and then falls to her knees.

The old woman's hands are lead. They fall to the ground. She digs her fingers into the pavement. Blood pricking through her skin. Wetting the border of her. She pushes her hands through the cement. She pushes down through the hole her own hands are making. She pushes down and down and down. Right down through the earth and out into the Atlantic. Her hands break through the ocean floor. Her fingers searching, reaching, in her mind, through the water, for whatever is left of her grandson's body after these twenty years.

Through the discordant la la refrain **Performer Three** *sings Hiondo Hionda, the song of the sea, calling the other voices to join her.*

7. The Sea

'Hiondo Hionda', the song of the sea swirls. **Performer One** *is back where we were when this all began.*

Performer One   The waves crash against the beach and she opens the bag for life. She looks down into the ashes.

They have formed a little clump on the top. She pushes her thumbnail into the clump expecting it to break apart like a ball of wet sand would but it doesn't. It is bone.

She cannot hold this anymore.

She looks up at the sea and she thinks of the wealth of suffering that *it* holds. The endlessness of it.

It is too much.

She cannot hold any of this.

She pulls the bag of ashes out of the bag for life and flings the contents out over the waves.

The wind carries clods and sprinkles of what was once body out across the water

'Hiondo Hionda' turns angry, ugly, unforgiving.

And the waves rise

And the waves crash

And the space between her and the dark clouds above

Squeezes and lifts

And squeezes and lifts

And it feels like the sea is trying to tell her something

But the words are muddled and impossible to understand

And she isn't sure she wants to know they have to say anyway

But it won't stop

The sea won't stop

And the clouds move across the sky

And the ocean moves across the land

Performer Two *starts to wail the opening refrain of the melody for 'Kilmarnock' in the same ugly, unforgiving tone, everyone joins in.*

The **Performers** *circle each other as the sound climaxes and then sink down into a circle as if in a tiny boat.*

8. Baby Two

The opening refrain to 'Kilmarnock' continues but hummed, lapping gentle and hopeful again.

Performer One   Remember the baby. Remember the baby. She is only a few hours old. She is on a small, crowded inflatable boat in the middle of the Mediterranean, being passed from stranger to stranger. She feels the boat shudder and the body that belongs to the arms that are holding her right now groans and tenses and she hears the sound of retching and then the roar of the waves as she feels her body being thrust into another pair of arms.

Performer Three   Back on the shore behind her, her mother sits and bleeds and watches the point on the horizon where the boat disappeared. Her mother's body shudders as her uterus shrinks back to the size it was before her. Her mother's breasts are solid, the nipples throbbing and oozing. Between her mother's legs the placenta lies like a meaty jellyfish dead on the shore. The umbilical chord reaching towards the ocean.

It is growing dark and the men who have brought her this far want her mother to go but her mother can't move. Soon. Soon her mother will begin to think about working towards another crossing. About finding the way to her older children. And maybe, one day, maybe finding her way back to her baby. There are networks. There are smart phones. There are stories.

But right now, as her mother sits bereft of the person she has shared her body with for the past nine months, all she wants is to be holding her baby as the boat carries them over the darkening horizon.

Performer One *reaches out to others surrounding her. Everyone stands facing inwards, together. A drone begins.*

Performer One   Think of that newborn baby, in that captain-less, crew-less boat, now being handed to yet another stranger who holds her tight with one arm and with the other grips two older children as the waves swirl around them.

Performer One *leads everyone in the singing of 'Always My Eyes' in the style of the singing of the psalms in Gaelic, to the tune of 'Kilmarnock'.*

ALWAYS MY EYES
Always my eyes
On the horizon
My children's hands in mine
We will not be shaken
We will not be shaken
Our trials are nearly done
Our trials are nearly done

We hold onto the final note. **Performer One** *calls everyone back to the story of the UN Worker with the 'oh hì, oh hò' refrain from 'Leis an Lurgainn'.*

9. Young Woman Two

Performer Five   Remember the young woman with scars on her wrists. Think of her now not on a beach in Mayanmar but walking along East 45th Street a few blocks in from UN HQ NYC. The blood of the massacre of a few days ago is completely absent from these sterile streets.

She thinks of how this job lets her be in one place and then the next like that. Transcending space, politics and time like magic. Like she's down-loaded a cheat code in the game of borders.

They decided she needed psychiatric treatment so here she is walking into this psychotherapist's office right now.

She holds out her right hand to greet the shrink and watches him clock the scars before shaking it. Start the timer. She thinks to herself. I'll give this silver fox five minutes before he's prodding into that pit of shit.

Performer One   So.

Performer Five   He says.

Performer One   You've been having a hard time.

Performer Five   She wants to say 'no shit, Sherlock'. She
wants to say 'Do you read the news?' She wants to say 'Do
you have any fucking idea?' But she doesn't say anything
and again his eyes rest on her wrists and she thinks now?
Now? He's going to ask now? She's not even been here for
two minutes! But he isn't asking now. He's asking something
else. Something about if she feels like no one understands
her? Like everything is awful and it's all her fault? Like
nothing she does will ever make anything, anywhere better?

And she imagines grabbing him by his silver man bun,
kneeing him in the balls and hurling him to the floor.

And now he's holding his pencil delicately between his
thumb and his forefinger and he's asking if she has trouble
sleeping? Trouble concentrating? Trouble maintaining
relationships?

And she wants to grab that pencil and stab it repeatedly into
his crystal blue eyes.

And now he's saying that PTSD, Post Traumatic Stress
Disorder is very common these days.

These days? These days? As if the thing this metrosexual
moron is calling PTSD hasn't been the standard state of
existence for most people in the world since forever.

And now she is thinking of her little brother. Just like she did
the other day after the massacre. Why is he always here in
her head? He was just a toddler. She barely even knew him.
She barely even remembers him.

And she is thinking about a story she heard on her gap year
about a fisherman many, many years ago who took his baby
in his fishing boat with him because his wife had died and no
else could take care of the thing. And how the fisherman had
left the baby on the shelf of a cave thinking it would be safe
but the sea swelled and the father got into the boat to save
himself and forgot about the baby. And how many days after
the wake, the father returned to the cave to find a mother

seal feeding what he thought was a baby seal only to discover his *own* child fighting fit on seal's milk.

The refrain from 'Leis an Lurgainn' turns weird and warped

Performer Five   And she thinks of her brother as he might be now, a strapping twenty-year-old seal boy living in some far flung corner of the world not yet ruined by humanity. And now the psychotherapist's eyes are looking very wet and sad indeed and she is imagining this psychotherapist as a seal being bludgeoned on a beautiful silver beach somewhere and calling for her brother the selkie to come and use the language of the humans to tell them to spare this man-bunned-psychotherapist-prick's life for he, with his perfectly manicured nose hair, is actually one of the good guys.

And now she is feeling a bit sick because all of this is really weird and she is wondering if she has said any of this out loud because the psychotherapist is telling her that he can see she is in deep trauma and is recommending she do something or other when she just stands up and walks out.

The soundscape stops completely. Everyone stands.

Performer Five   And she walks down the stairs. And she walks out into the sunshine. And she wants to call her mum. And her gran. But she can't. And she pushes open the door of a travel agent. And she holds her credit card out in her pointless hands with their stupid, scarred wrists. And she buys a ticket on the next flight to where her she knows her hands will be useful.

Performer Four *stands and lets out an ululation, everyone joins in and we all spin around as* **Performer Four** *sings a Basque chant about the women who were burnt as witches during the Spanish Inquisition.*

> SORGINA
> Erre zenituzten sorginen ilobak gera gu

The **Performers** *spin out and find themselves kneeling again, gently singing the 'Mwanangu La La' refrain.*

12. Old Woman Three

Performer Four *remains central, embodying the old woman.*

Performer Two   Remember the old woman who can't speak English. Think of her now sitting in a hospital bed with her fingers bandaged up. She looks down at her phone and tries to swipe the screen but the bandages are too tight. Why is she wearing these stupid things? What on earth is she doing here? Where is her daughter?

Performer Three   'Mamá?'

Performer Two   She hears. A drained and anxious face peers around the curtain. It's a pleasant face. Tired eyes. The person walks in and perches on the bed beside her. She holds out the phone towards the person.

Performer Four   Por favor, llamen a mi hija?

Performer Two   She asks and the woman's tired eyes prick with tears. The woman says

Performer Three   'I am your daughter, Mamá.'

Performer Two   She looks back at the phone and jabs a bandage at the screen again . . . and jabs a bandage at the screen again. The tired eyed woman gently takes the phone, opens the screen and holds a picture up and says

Performer Three   Ves Mamá? Soy yo.

Performer Four   The old woman reaches out for the phone and searches the photos. There are pictures of the woman with the tired eyes and now some pictures of a much younger woman who looks like them both who has scars on her wrists. The old woman keeps looking through the photos. The tired eyed woman ask

Performer Three   A quién buscas?

Performer Two   And she says:

Performer Four   Dónde está el niño?

Performer Two   The old woman doesn't notice the tired eyed woman go pale. She just keeps flipping through the photos looking for the boy. He must be about twenty now. With bony shoulders and wide cheekbones and deep dark eyes like his uncles. On the other side of the curtain there is a machine that breathes and sighs. It sounds like the sea. A nurse walks by and the tired eyed woman jumps up to follow her and thankfully the old woman is alone again. Alone with her phone and the sound of the sea from the other side of the curtain.

The old woman closes her eyes and remembers sitting on the beach near where she grew up in Colombia. She remembers the sun warming her skin, the waves licking her toes and the horizon stretching out to forever. She remembers feeling like anything was possible. Like the whole world was at the tips of her fingers as long as the sun was shining and the ocean was twirling its continual dazzling dance.

Performer Four *and* **Performer Three** *sing 'Mwanangu La La' together, harmonising, mournful, yet hopeful.*

Performer Two   She remembers diving into the sea's endless blue. She remembers the crackling of salt against her scalp. She remembers the excitement just before taking a deep breath and diving down into it. She remembers the feeling of touching her toes on the cool sand on the ocean floor and looking up at the circle of light far above her.

She remembers the feeling inside her lungs when they start bursting for air. She remembers twirling her fingers through the water as she pushes up towards the surface. She remembers that final moment of doubt before reaching the surface and the burst of joy when her head breaks the waves and her lungs fill with air and looking back at the golden sand of home. Colombia.

Performer Two *sings the 'oh hì, oh hò' refrain from 'Leis an Lurgainn' and everyone joins in returning to the story of the UN Worker.*

13. Young Woman Three

Performer Five   Remember the young woman with the scars on her wrists. Think of her opening the zip of the tent she has put up a little back from a beach on the island of Lesbos. The magic of credit cards and diplomatic passports and air miles and other cheat codes and here she is. She has been here less than twenty-four hours and already her arms feel like lead and she feels like it is going to take a fork lift truck to move her. And then she sees them out on the water and her hands are pushing her up and out and she is running with everyone else and they are all calling

Performer Four/Performer Three/Performer One/ Performer Two   Por acqui! / Tenemos agua y comida! / Bijo Invar! / We are with the Red Cross!

The 'oh hì, oh hò' refrain from 'Leis an Lurgainn' evolves gradually into the gentle wash of 'leis' and 'seòl'.

Performer Five   And the boat comes closer in and she is running into the waves with her feet and her legs fizzing with the rush of another chance. And then they are here. Wet. Cold. Scared. Bodies. Faces. Eyes. Hands. Arms reaching for her through the darkness.

And now a pair of hands is thrusting a body into her arms. A tiny, silent body, all scrunched up and frozen.

She feels the weight of this new born baby's body in her scarred arms and suddenly she remembers her gran once telling her that it is only when you hold a new born baby that you remember what arms are really for.

And the waves are pushing the backs of her knees and sucking at the sand between her toes and now her hands are rubbing the tiny, frozen chest. Rubbing and rubbing and rubbing it. And time slows to a standstill and the only things moving are her hands and the waves. Her hands rubbing that tiny frozen chest. Rubbing and rubbing and rubbing it. And the waves swirling around them both.

And it's weird but she feels like voices are bubbling up through the water from the ocean floor.

And now her clothes begin to swirl as the waves lick her waist and reach for that frozen new born baby. And even though her hands with those stupid scarred wrists are rubbing this baby's tiny frozen chest – rubbing and rubbing and rubbing it – she can't move the rest of her.

Performers One, **Two**, **Three** *and* **Four** *keen.*

And suddenly she is five years old and she is chasing her little brother along the corridors of the ship. And they are laughing. And now they are out on deck and she is gripping him by his tummy and swinging him around and around. And now they are rolling on the slippery floor of the deck and she is covering his cheeks with kisses. And now he is squealing and wriggling away. And now he is climbing. And now she is watching him climb up, up, up to the railing. And now she can see that he is going to fall over the side of the ship. And now she is saying to her body to get up off the deck and go to him and pull him back to safety. But her stupid arms, her stupid legs, her stupid body won't move.

And now her mother and gran are beside her. And now her mother is holding onto the railing and reaching down to the waves far below and her crying sounds like the howling of the wind. And now her gran is shaking her and shouting. Shouting at her. Screaming in her face. Screaming and screaming and screaming.

Only now, in her mind, this time, she is the one who has fallen into the sea.

Performers One, Two, Three *and* **Four** *close in on* **Performer Five**, *as if they are the sea.* **Performer Five** *emerges, changed, cleansed, reborn.* **Performer One** *leads everyone in singing the glorious gospel song 'Deep Blue Sea', softly at first then growing with vitality, encouraging the audience to join in.*

DEEP BLUE SEA
Deep Blue Sea, Baby, Deep Blue Sea (3x)
It was sister what got drowned in the Deep Blue Sea

Dig her grave with a silver spade (3x)
It was sister what got drowned in the Deep Blue Sea

Deep Blue Sea, Baby, Deep Blue Sea (3x)
It was sister what got drowned in the Deep Blue Sea

Golden sun bring her back to me (3x)
It was sister what got drowned in the Deep Blue Sea

Deep Blue Sea, Baby, Deep Blue Sea (3x)
It was sister what got drowned in the Deep Blue Sea
It was sister what got drowned in the . . . Deep . . . Blue
. . . Sea

15. Baby Three

The **Performers** *return to the hopeful refrain of 'Kilmarnock' this time hummed fully, in unison, in harmony.*

Performer One   Remember the new born baby. Think of her skin, only a few hours old. Think of it beginning to tingle as a stranger's hands rubs it. Think of the warmth from those hands spreading through her tiny new born body. Think of her tiny new born mouth opening and gulping air into her tiny lungs. Think of her tiny body being lifted high over the waves by arms that have a weave of scars running across the wrists. Think of that stranger with the scarred wrists leaping over the waves holding the new born baby up high and shouting

Performer Five   This baby is alive!

Performer Four   And now think of what the baby hears. She hears the thud of bare feet on sand. She hears a voice that she doesn't know is her own crying. She hears the beating heart of the stranger as she is held close to her chest and the stranger shouts

Performer Five   This baby is alive!

Performer Two   And now this stranger is carrying her into a tent and the air grows heavy and thick. And there is shouting and weeping and talking and beeping and bright, white light all around and the baby cries but this stranger's hands are still holding her. And now lights are shone in her eyes and her nose and her ears and cold, hard, sharp things pressed against her and into her and there is beeping and there is light everywhere and the stranger's hands are still holding her.

Performer Five   This baby is alive.

Performer Three   And now something warm and whole and good is dropped on the baby's tongue. And she wraps her lips around a bottle and drinks and drinks and drinks and drinks and drinks. And she opens her eyes and it is light and the stranger is looking down at her. And the baby stops drinking. And this stranger smiles. And then the baby opens her tiny mouth again and cries and screams and howls.

Performer Five   And as the stranger with the scars on her wrists holds the baby she thinks of her own mother holding her as a baby. And she thinks of her own grand mother holding her mother as baby before that. And she thinks of her own babies who she has not yet had, and might never have. And she thinks of the babies who have been lost like her brother. And she thinks aren't all of these children all of our children anyway. And she remembers a voice telling her that it is only when you hold a new born baby that you remember what arms are really for. And as she holds this crying, screaming, howling new born being, she knows what her hands, and her scarred arms are really for. And she knows that she has to see her mum. She has to see her mum. And she has to see her gran. Soon. Really, really soon.

Performer Two   And back in Scotland it is the middle of the night and the stranger's gran wakes up with a jolt and looks around her to find that she is no longer in hospital but tucked up in bed safe at home in Glasgow. And everything comes flooding back to her. Everything that she hasn't been able to remember for what feels like forever comes flooding back to her. And part of her wants to call out to her daughter in the next room to find out what on earth is going on. And another part of her wants to just sit still and hold on to everything she can remember before it all leaves again. And another part of her, the biggest part of her wants to find her phone and call her granddaughter and tell her how happy she is that she is alive.

Performer One   And the baby screams

and the stranger with the scars on her wrists remembers a song her gran learnt not so long ago about telling a baby to sleep like the fishies at the bottom of the sea

and the baby cries

and the stranger doesn't know the words to the song or even really the melody

and the baby cries

but the stranger sings it anyway

Performer Five *begins to sing 'Mwanangu La La' gently, awkwardly, brightly.*

Performer One   and the baby's cries turn to whimpers

and the stranger sways

and the baby's eyes begin to close

and the stranger moves

and the baby's breath deepens

and the stranger holds her

and the baby sleeps.

The sound gives way to 'Hiondo Hionda' and everything returns, once again to the start.

Epilogue

The ritual resumes. The singing gently ebbs away to silence and one by one the **Performers** *disappear until only* **Performer One** *is left.*

Performer One   She stands, her white toes pressing into the sand of the beach,

She stands.

And she thinks of all the lives that have been lost to the sea as the continual cycle of people buffeted across it by forces within and outwith their control continues.

She looks at the sea.

She can see no trace of the ashes of the body she once loved.

Just sea.

Just ocean.

That has no words.

No stories.

No eyes.

No thoughts.

No feelings.

No face.

No memories.

No voice.

No solace.

No torment.

A body of water.

And salt.

And sand.

And sound.

And life.

And death.

A border.

Rising.

And falling.

And rising.

And falling.

And rising.

And rising.

And rising.

Every day.

She stands.

And the space between her toes and the waves shrinks
and grows.

She stands.

And the space between them shrinks

And grows.

She stands.

And the space

shrinks

and grows

and shrinks

and grows

and shrinks

and grows . . .

End.

www.ingramcontent.com/pod-product-compliance
Ingram Content Group UK Ltd.
Pitfield, Milton Keynes, MK11 3LW, UK
UKHW020706280225
455688UK00012B/289